THE ...
AND YOUR
EVERYDAY LIFE

Ronda Chervin, Ph.D.

LIGUORI
PUBLICATIONS

One Liguori Drive
Liguori, Mo. 63057
(314) 464-2500

Imprimi Potest:
Edmund T. Langton, C.SS.R.
Provincial, St. Louis Province
Redemptorist Fathers

Imprimatur:
+ Charles R. Koester
Vicar General, Archidocese of St. Louis

TABLE OF CONTENTS

INTRODUCTION

Suppose you walked into a room in your home and found it dark and dull and depressing. Would you leave it that way? Not if you planned to spend any time there. To change the atmosphere you could probably turn the lights on, then, perhaps, play some lively music.

To apply this analogy to our daily life, when most of us look seriously at the *way we spend our time, the attitude we have toward our work, and the character of our conversation,* we are depressed at what we see. Somehow we have allowed these conditions to grow. We are caught in quicksand. And strangely, we find such lack of resistance quite natural. Natural, yes! Holy, no! God does not want these conditions to exist. They are a departure from the faith, hope, and love which should always be the major ingredients of a Christian's interior life.

We must yield our wrong attitudes to the Holy Spirit; let him pull us out of the quicksand so we can lift our hearts to God in praise again.

Returning to the analogy of the dark room, the following pages will show us how the graces of the Holy Spirit correspond to the lights and the music that were used to brighten up the dull exterior surroundings.

The Light

The light of the Holy Spirit is given to us in the gifts of discernment and counsel. These gifts are not only to be applied to high spiritual matters but also to the analysis of our own daily life situations and experiences. The spiritual graces aid our natural reasoning power which is often in bondage to our wrong attitudes.

In our tranquilizer-society we have grown accustomed to believing most sickness can be dissolved by appropriate drugs, and surely there are times when they can be a real godsend. But in the Spirit we discover that a more powerful cure is needed: the cleansing grace of God.

The disorders caused by our wrong attitudes in daily life can cause a constant negative pall to settle over our souls. A person who gives all his attention to work and almost none to his family will naturally feel depressed each evening as he returns to his neglected home. He knows that he has done nothing to water the garden of his home relationships, and the weeds that have grown up instead of flowers are depressing to observe. There is no way in which he can overcome these conditions until he yields his family life up for spiritual renewal and at the same time offers his own mind, heart, and soul to his family in a ministry of love.

The Music

What corresponds to the music which brightens up the atmosphere of a dull room? The song which the Holy Spirit would sing with us is made of several elements:

Understanding the causes of our wrong attitudes is the *opening theme.* The lively rebuking of these conditions as unworthy of a child of God is the "music" of the Spirit which *crescendos* as it overcomes our slavery to wrong attitudes.

The peaceful *adagio* is the return of the soul to the place of peace to be with Christ. Here deep in the heart of the Lord we realize what we need, what is important and what unimportant; and, in contrition, we see what we must change in our life style that is sinful or disordered. In prayer the Lord may give us the courage to seek the help we need instead of pretending that "all is well" while sinking deeper and deeper into our wrong attitudes.

The music of the Spirit then bursts forth in the *victory theme,* as we rejoice in his saving power, renew our gratitude for all the good gifts in our lives, praise the Lord, and spread his love by reaching out with little deeds of love to those around us.

CHAPTER ONE

YOUR DAY
IN THE SPIRIT

"How do you spend your time?"

This is an innocuous-looking question asked over and over again, yet it reveals a very special relationship to time: one of possession. The image of time that many of us have is that it *belongs to us.* Some of the hours of the day we commit to work for the sake of survival, and some we consider as chore time which we give in exchange for other services — the rest is ours to use as we want.

How simple and natural is such a view of time, and yet how completely contrary to the image of time the Christian should have!

How so? The religious person knows that time belongs to God. It is given to us in trusteeship. The day ahead is but a portion of the "life-time" that God gives to us for a purpose: to build the kingdom of love on earth and ready ourselves more and more for heaven by opening ourselves to God's love and love of neighbor.

Accordingly, the first question a Christian should ask about any parcel of time should be, "What is your will, my God?" and now "What can I do with my time?" We should always be in the position of Mary saying, "Behold the handmaid of the Lord, be it done unto me according to thy will" (Lk 1:38).

Ideally the Christian prays constantly. Each activity of the day is inserted into the total gift of his mind and heart and soul to God. If we have never quite conceived of our time in this way, it would be desirable to yield up to the Holy Spirit each of the main ways we spend our time. We should not be confused or anxious about such a proposal. Instead we should go to the place of peace with Christ and listen to his loving plans for us.

There are various ways of categorizing the activities with which we fill our waking time. Here is one way of dividing it. (As you go through the list you can note what activities of your own days fall under each category and approximately how much time a day you spend on each. A notation may differ from individual to individual. For example, a person who loves to cook would list this activity under creativity, whereas another person would put it under work. Mealtimes for some involve personal communication; for others they are but time spent in a necessary activity.

8

a) Indispensable work
b) Habitual extra work
c) Personal, loving communication
d) Wasteful or un-Christian talk
e) Creative activities
f) Loving recreation
g) Dissipating entertainment
h) Time alone
i) Prayer, liturgical worship, ministries

I will examine each category and briefly discuss some Christian attitudes toward it. Later the topic of priorities and scheduling in terms of growth in the Spirit will be discussed.

Instead of postponing the exercises until the end of the chapter, I suggest that you read this section very slowly and open yourself to the challenges, encouragements, and inspirations of the Spirit.

a) and b) Indispensable work and *Habitual extra work.* For most of us indispensable work would include what we do to earn a living, the time taken to get there, study for a career, or housework. The Christian ought to accept such work as part of the human condition and also a way for serving himself and those he loves by supplying what is needed for physical sustenance. Work which is directly concerned with helping people would also fall under the category of ministry which will be considered later.

Assuming that a great deal of the work we do for wages is not ministerial but simply a way to earn enough money to survive, the question of what is indispensable work becomes an issue which itself ought to be yielded to the Spirit. Nothing has to be! St. Francis of Assisi witnessed to the whole world once and forever how little was needed to live if one was really living in the Spirit. I think it would be beneficial for each one of us to go to the place of peace with Christ and talk to him about our needs and see what he wants us to have and how much work is necessary to attain this.

For example, suppose a man is working on a job which requires eight hours a day and an average of three hours a day overtime, in order to support a standard of living in which prime cuts of meat are served every night, the baby has a toy box filled to the brim, the older kids get a new bicycle every Christmas, and his wife can hardly find the particular dress she is looking for because the closet is so full. Assuming that this father's work has no special value in terms of helping the community, it would seem that his overtime work is not really indispensable to living a Christian life with his family. It is only necessary for leading a life of affluence such as has never been recommended to Christians anyhow.

Sometimes parents justify much overtime work because of the expenses of college education; but this goal must also be yielded to the Spirit since very often the real reason for sending the young person to the expensive college is not so that he can learn wisdom or become a better Christian but rather so that he can attain a certain desirable status in the world. Here we can easily see the development of a vicious legacy: The father has no time to spend with his children in loving fellowship and Christian prayer because he is so busy working to achieve status and wealth to send them to school; then they can get positions in society which will make demands on their time which exclude time spent in love of God and neighbor in favor of competition — and so on down through the generations.

If we turn to the subject of housework, we find also that yielding our habits of work to the Spirit enables us to discover a freedom we did not know we had. Just to focus on but one example: If all members of the family are allowed to throw their clothing into the hamper each night, then the housewife has to do a wash or two every day. If all are encouraged to remove their good clothing when they come home and don jeans or housedresses, then this woman would have a wash only once every third day! Having the older children do their own wash and ironing would probably insure two thirds less housework for mother.

This may sound more like common sense than spiritual wisdom. Where does the Holy Spirit come into such a decision? We will see this later on when we come to priorities. A person who enters more and more into relationships of deep love of God and

10

of family and neighbor will want to spend less time on any dispensable work and more time on what directly serves to build the kingdom of love. This is one of the many meanings, I think, of the famous rebuke of Jesus to Martha: "Now as they went on their way, he entered a village; and a woman named Martha received him into her house. And she had a sister called Mary, who sat at the Lord's feet and listened to his teaching. But Martha was distracted with much serving; and she went to him and said, 'Lord, do you not care that my sister has left me to serve alone? Tell her then to help me.' But the Lord answered her, 'Martha, Martha, you are anxious and troubled about many things; one thing is needful. Mary has chosen the good portion, which shall not be taken from her' " (Lk 10: 38-42).

c) and d) Personal loving communication and Wasteful or un-Christian talk. Friendship is a great gift of God. I think it would be disastrous to exclude conversation in favor of constant work. Fathers and mothers should often have time to talk to their children in a friendly unhurried manner. But lots of time is spent in conversation that is simply a waste of time. Instead of yielding our time to the Spirit we may yield it to whichever neighbor or office buddy passes by and wants to talk. It must be a bitter experience for a child to find that the same mother who one moment before claims she is too busy to discuss her child's problems will be ready to talk for an hour on the phone about trivial matters to an acquaintance! Perhaps the child becomes so used to this kind of double-talk that he stops communicating all together with his parents. Sometimes we are really yielding the time to the Evil One when the time is spent in an especially uncharitable way because it is filled with mean gossip or with arguments.

e) Creative activities. The Lord gives each one of us special talents. He wants us to use them. An artist, Jacqui Taylor, while lecturing on Creativity and the Holy Spirit, once said that if we feel a deep desire to do something creative, even if we haven't a shred of confidence in our ability to do it, the urge could be the result of the promptings of the Holy Spirit. God is a creator and we are

11

made in his image. We should not judge our creativity by stand-ards of others. We should yield to the Spirit. Perhaps trying this particular activity we have always wanted to do will make us very happy. Maybe a picture I make of my own garden, which I show to no one else, will help me to discover the beauty of the trees and flowers in my own backyard and lead me to praise God for each of them as part of my future prayer life.

f) and g) Loving recreation and Dissipating entertainment. Some Christians think that the ideal of serious religious life yielded to the Spirit is work and prayer with no time wasted in recreation. Quite the contrary! Throughout the ages we find that even the strictest monastic orders in the Church always include recreation as part of the rule. It is necessary for our growth in the Spirit to praise God by enjoying his gifts of nature, good food, entertain-ment, and the company of each other. Happy recreation can be a foretaste of heaven in its release from labor, worry, and productiv-ity, for the sake of loving fellowship. Families which have no place for having fun together often come to see each other more as functionaries in the work of the house than as delightful, if often difficult, companions.

But, of course, there is another kind of recreation or entertain-ment which is negative. When we participate in this type of fun we really let go of the Holy Spirit to enjoy worldly values without the embarrassment of taking along our usual moral standards. How else can we explain this fact? Normally we consider sexual in-nuendos, foolish talk, underhand shrewdness or fraud to be sinful, but given a few drinks at a certain kind of party, or a relaxed mood in front of a smart, witty talk-show, and we are ready to laugh as if sin were delightful and the good was stuffy or phony or naïve.

One way to distinguish the two types of recreation is to see if it is really possible to let Christ be our companion during this particular time of relaxation. In the case of good, loving, recrea-tion we can praise the Lord with great delight for each good thing we are experiencing from the sunshine, the trees, the animals, the friends, the children, as well as the food and wine. In the case of un-Christian recreation we have to try to pretend we aren't Christians in order to enjoy it!

h) Time alone. I think that the Holy Spirit wants to lead us into solitude from time to time, not to make us feel lonely but so that we can experience Christ's love for us as individuals as well as participants in a community. Even though it is he who leads us into close bonds of love with others, there is a part of each human soul that no one knows but God. Even Jesus used to leave the multitude and go off by himself to pray.

Especially if a person is suffering from a feeling of pressure or conflict, it is desirable to spend time alone with God with no other purpose but to be one's own self and experience God's blessing.

i) Prayer, liturgical worship, ministries. As we so well know, the Spirit is leading us to constant prayer. Just as we think over everything that happens to us in our own minds, we should share it in loving converse with the Lord, for he is truly present to us. Such prayer does not entail loss of attention to what we are doing. It is an accompaniment, just as we can do many things with music playing in the room. We should also have definite times when we concentrate exclusively on prayer, worship, and ministering to others in the Lord. To fail to do so actually amounts to saying to Christ "Work, people, driving, sports, and TV are worthy of my exclusive attention, but you are not!"

As described in more detail in the first booklet of this series, *Prayer and Your Everyday Life,* I think that the Holy Spirit has always led the People of God into prayer on arising, attendance at a daily liturgical worship service, when possible, little islands of prayer during the day, a time of silent prayer of at least 10 to 15 minutes, and an evening prayer and spiritual reading. Certain prayers are especially suitable for groups of friends or for families: lighting a candle and having people read Scripture in turn either day by day following the order of the Bible or each one opening the Scripture and reading at random; reading sections of the Divine Office (now called *Liturgy of the Hours);* simple movement or dance to prayers such as the *Our Father or Hail Mary;* praying the Rosary or Stations of the Cross; lighting a candle on the table before dinner and praying while holding hands, adding prayer intentions after grace is said. Blessing each other by placing the hands over the heads of each person in the group or family and praying over them as each one leaves the house or before bed can be done by parents and children. Some children like to be sprinkled with Holy Water, or to have the sign of the cross made on the forehead. It is good to try out such prayerful practices as thanking God each evening after dinner for what is good in each person in the family or prayer community, or for special graces of the day. Some reply to the question "How did you see Christ in each person during the day?" Delightful ways to celebrate great religious holidays can be found in booklets on seasonal prayer. (See *Advent Begins at Home* and *Lent Begins at Home,* Liguori Publications booklets.)

We should be available at some time during the week for helping others as a ministry of the Lord. This can take any number of forms. It may be praying with someone, counseling a person who needs advice in the family or neighborhood, teaching Christian doctrine to people in the family, parish, or Sunday School; it may be a time of intercessory prayer for others, prayers for healing, doing work that aids the poor, working on a right-to-life hotline, helping on a social action program to improve institutions in the country which impede justice. Such activities are truly ministries rather than merely work we were trapped into by eager committee women or by a bad conscience — if we do them for Christ, at the leading of the Spirit, with the prayers of the community, and in a spirit of constant openness to witnessing to the Lord's power rather than our own.

Priorities

Given the fact that we open ourselves in prayer to the Spirit and yield to him in the concrete by considering the different activities of our day and seeing what we are doing, several main questions arise: "How can I decide what is more important to do? Should I increase some and decrease others? How rigid or flexible should my schedule be?"

From the way the categories of activities have been described, it is pretty clear that under most circumstances the Christian ought to try to increase times spent in personal communication with family and friends, creative activities, good recreation, time alone, and prayerful activities. This can be done by finding ways to do indispensable work more efficiently (it is amazing how quickly work that one thought would take many hours can be done if something exciting to do demands speedy accomplishment), and by gradually decreasing time spent on busy work, wasteful and un-Christian talk, and dissipating entertainment.

Such a prescription sounds so obvious that we wonder why all persons do not simply leap in and reorganize their lives accordingly. I think we are so reluctant to do so because we lack confidence in the power of the Spirit to make the good activities truly enjoyable. Sometimes deep personal conversations make us happy, but there is the risk of getting in over our heads; we may feel drawn to a particular area of creativity but we fear that we are kidding ourselves and that we are not good enough to dare to do it; we know that once we get started, wholesome recreation can be lots of fun, but there is more effort involved in going on a hike or even to the local beach than in flipping on the TV. We know that Jesus wants to meet us in prayer and especially in the sacraments, but since we don't always feel like going to the depth within ourselves where we do experience him, it is easier to dwell on a more superficial level.

What we have to realize is that the very nature of our selfhood is at stake in the choices we make about time. Shall we become what God dreams we may be, by following the lead of the Spirit, or shall we simply remain comfortable yet empty?

Perhaps you might reply, "I don't hear the Spirit calling me into new activities." Very often the voice of God is the still small sound which gradually lures us through the years by its melody. Certainly no book could set a timetable for the reader which would predict on what day, month, and year he would feel called to change this segment of his life. But sometimes the voice is very clear, and we cannot hear it because our schedule is too crowded with nonessentials for us to have time for what God wants us to do. For example, if a woman has it fixed in her mind that she must

15

play bridge with the neighborhood women every morning of the week, then she could not accept a ministry of social work which involves appearing on the job at 9 a.m. each morning.

Schedules

This brings us to the question of rigidity, flexibility, and openness to the Spirit. At the extremes, some people have the day divided almost moment by moment. Others float free doing what they feel like at any moment, easily breaking appointments if something more fruitful seems to come along. In neither case does such an attitude toward schedules appear to be especially spiritual. The man with the rigid schedule may make an idol of his own agenda. The man who glorifies freedom may be really rejecting clear duties.

It seems to me that a key concept in determining the degree of fidelity we should have to a schedule is the commitment of prime time (hours when we are wide awake and full of energy) to certain good activities, and the importance of making such times the backbone of the schedule. For example, we may decide that we need to have a definite prime time in our weekly schedule for friendship or for being alone with a girl friend or wife or for creative activity or for prayer. We may decide that we can do our indispensable work more efficiently if we make a rather tight schedule for it, thus freeing us from nagging anxiety about unfinished work during times of leisure. Many students find that if they schedule definite times for pure study in the library without benefit of radio, stereo, TV, or chats with passing friends, then they can really enjoy recreation time without any worries about finishing assignments in the middle of the night.

We have to realize that — in our busy modern world — failure to schedule time for an activity means most often neglecting it. The father who does not plan outings with the children will probably be drawn into household chores during his limited weekend time at home. The family which has no time set aside for prayer with the children — leaving it up to chance — will find that they hardly ever experience the warmth, peace, and spiritual sharing which comes from a time in each day when everyone joins together in the Lord in spite of all distractions, sacrifices, and hassles.

On the other hand, we cannot follow the Holy Spirit day by day if we are never willing to depart from our schedule to respond to circumstances. Failure to be flexible can be a very serious difficulty in the life of a highly organized person. Arbitrary deadlines can become sources of enormous pressure. Eruptions of temper follow any circumstance that breaks into the plan.

The fact that I am doing a good thing, which I am sure about because I prayed over it five years ago and decided it was God's will, does not mean that today the Spirit may not be calling me to a new vocation or a totally different deadline which would free me for other very important activities.

On the day-to-day level — a man busy at work gets a call saying that his child was in an accident. He might reason that since his wife is with the child she will take care of everything, and he need not leave his very important meeting. But the Holy Spirit may be leading him to put aside the meeting and be by his wife's side to show love for the child who is feeling so vulnerable, and to pray with his wife for healing. God writes the script of life, not we. Since God gives us our time we must always be ready to yield it back to him.

Yearly retreats or days of recollection provide us with a good way to yield our time up again wholly to the Spirit. The advice of friends, family, and of a spiritual director can show us in what ways the Lord might be calling us to a reallocation of time for greater ministry in the kingdom, or to rebuke us if we may be squandering time in un-Christian ways, or becoming rigid and not hearing the call of the Spirit in situations which arise.

SUGGESTED PRAYER EXERCISES

Reexamine this whole section slowly and ask the Holy Spirit to rebuke, inspire, and encourage you in terms of the way the passages relate to your own life.

PASSAGES FROM SCRIPTURE

"For everything there is a season, and a time for every matter under heaven . . . a time to seek, and a time to lose; a time to keep, and a time to cast away, a time to keep silence, and a time to speak. . . . I have seen the business that God has given to the sons of men to be busy with. He has made everything beautiful in its time; also he has put eternity into man's mind, yet so that he cannot find out what God has done from the beginning to the end. I know that there is nothing better for them than to be happy and enjoy themselves as long as they live; also that it is God's gift to man that everyone should eat and drink and take pleasure in all his labor" (Eccl 3:1-6, 7, 10-13).

"But take heed to yourselves lest your hearts be weighed down with dissipation and drunkenness and cares of this life, and that day come upon you suddenly like a snare, for it will come upon all who dwell upon the face of the whole earth. But watch at all times, praying that you may have strength to escape all these things that will take place, and to stand before the Son of man" (Lk 21:34-36).

" 'Take heed and beware of all covetousness; for a man's life does not consist in the abundance of his possessions.' And he told them a parable saying 'The land of a rich man brought forth plentifully; and he thought to himself, 'What shall I do, for I have nowhere to store my crops?' And he said, 'I will do this: I will pull down my barns, and build larger ones; and there I will store all my grain and my goods. And I will say to my soul, Soul, you have ample goods laid up for many years; take your ease, eat, drink and be merry.' But God said to him, 'Fool! This night your soul is required of you; and the things you have prepared, whose will they be?' So is he who lays up treasure for himself, and is not rich towards God' " (Lk 12:15-21).

"Provide yourselves with purses that do not grow old, with a treasure in the heavens that does not fail, where no thief approaches and no moth destroys. For where your treasure is, there will your heart be also" (Lk 12:33-34).

"Look carefully then how you walk, not as unwise men but as wise, making the most of the time, because the days are evil. Therefore do not be foolish, but understand what the will of the Lord is" (Eph 5:15-17).

"Make every effort to supplement your faith with virtue, and virtue with knowledge, and knowledge with self-control, and self-control with steadfastness, and steadfastness with godliness, and godliness with brotherly affection, and brotherly affection with love" (2 Pt 1:5-7).

CHAPTER TWO

YOUR WORK
IN THE SPIRIT

For most adults more than one half the waking hours of the day are spent in work. How many of us exclude Christ from this time, except for a perfunctory offering at the start of the day? When we try to live our work life apart from the influence of the Holy Spirit we usually find that we fall into at least one of these four main unhappy relationships:

Work experienced as a scarcely tolerable burden.

Work that is ambition-directed and greed-oriented.

Work as a place of irritation, harsh criticism, wrangling, group in-fighting.

Indecision about what work to do in view of a deeper conversion to Christ.

Let us describe the way each of these attitudes toward work feels in terms of the description of a person involved, followed by the invitation of the Holy Spirit to meet Christ in a new way in those situations.

A. Work As a Burden

Paula is a housewife with several young children. She wakes up each morning to a scream from the youngest one to be taken out of his crib, and to the sounds of the wrangling of the older children in the kitchen. She mutters a hasty offering of the day's work to God and stumbles into the baby's room to begin an unending round of repetitious activities: changing diapers, making beds, scrubbing floors, cooking meals, cleaning messes, and being at the constant disposal of husband and children for their every need.

Paula is physically and emotionally exhausted. She finds herself continually yelling at the kids for causing so much dirt and disorder, muttering when the baby makes a mess in his diaper; being resentful of her husband's right to walk out the door each morning and not return till six.

Weekends are even worse. She still remembers when Saturday and Sunday had something to do with rest, but for her it is always more work. Her husband is home more, not helping but making demands on her or being annoyed that she is so cranky. The older children who are in school during the week spend the weekend

22

running in and out followed by groups of friends, raiding the refrigerator, and leaving their messes behind.

Paula finds it very hard to pray at Mass on Sunday after the fuss of getting the kids all clean and ready, bustling them into the car, and keeping them quiet during the service.

At her wit's end, Paula decided to take one day off and go for a walk on the beach and think about her life and how to accept it better. During the drive to the beach she finds herself repeating over and over to herself: "I can't stand it any more. I just can't stand it. I'm going to just run away or walk into the deep water and never be seen again. Let them all take care of themselves!"

She gets to the beach and begins to walk quickly along the shoreline, too angry to see the beauty of the ocean or to hear the "still small voice" of the Spirit trying to talk to her. Finally she slows down and says "O Lord, help me! Have mercy on me. You know I want to be a good wife and mother but this is slavery. Tell me what to do."

A voice in her heart says: "Dear, dear Paula. You work so hard for your family. I know that and I love you for it. If I would look only at your great effort, I would number you among my holy ones, but there is something deeply lacking in your life — joy! You have lost the joy you had in me when you were a young girl. Do you remember how you used to delight in everything I had made? Do you remember how you used to do every task out of love for me and for your husband and children. You are so weary, my child, because you no longer do your work with me."

I imagine that Jesus wants to draw all family people into the life of his Mother, Mary, and his father, Joseph. They worked in his presence and they learned many secrets from him. I picture Jesus as a young boy loving to watch his mother preparing vegetables. He would show her the beauty of each creation which had been made through him by his heavenly Father and she would rejoice in it, also. Look at so common a vegetable as an onion! How many onions have passed through the hands of a housewife? Did you ever take the time to really look at one? Robert F. Capon wrote in his book called the *Supper of the Lamb,* a theological cookbook, about the hidden beauty of the onion. Here are some excerpts from this remarkable piece:

(If you take an actual onion out of the cupboard and look at it, you will better understand what he means.)

"Try to look at it as if you had never seen an onion before . . . stand your onion root end down upon the board and see it as the pattern of life that it is — as one member of the vast living, gravity-defying troop that, across the face of the earth, moves light-and-airward as long as the world lasts. . . .

"Lift the skin with the point of your knife so as not to cut or puncture the flesh beneath . . . Look now at the fall of stripped and flaked skin before you. It is dry. It is, all things considered, one of the driest things in the world. . . it is of two colors: the outside a brownish yellow of no particular brightness; but the inside a soft, burnished, coppery gold, ribbed — especially near the upper end — with an exquisiteness only hinted at on the outside . . . it presents itself to you as the animals to Adam: as nameless till seen by man, to be met, known and christened into the city of being. It comes as a deputy of all the hiddennesses of the world, of all the silent competencies endlessly at work deep down in things. And they come to you — to you as their priest and voice, for oblation by your heart's astonishment at their great glory."

The Holy Spirit might invite Paula to try to see everything she works with in such an imaginative way. Look at the beauty of the wood in the furniture. Look at the colors in the clothing of your children and love them.

The Spirit also invites us to thank God for the gift of the things that we work with — the utensils, the foods, the chairs and tables. As St. Francis called the sun and moon "brother" and "sister" so we could say to all that surrounds us: "Praise the Lord for Sister washing machine which saves me so much work. . . ."

The Voice continues to speak to Paula about her work: "I do not send work to you merely as a punishment for the deeds of Adam and Eve but because I saw that through work you would be able to participate in the building of a world of love around your children. As you do each job in the house, consciously offer it out of love for each person. Pray for your husband as you iron his shirts, for the baby as you diaper him, for the older children as you straighten up after them.

"More than anything else, my daughter, I would like you to talk to me all day as you work. Do it with me. Say 'Jesus, I am happy to be with you today; let's do something beautiful for God together.' When you are too tired to talk, play a record of songs about the kingdom of God so that I can minister to you through my musicians. Steal a few minutes in a room away from the children and just sink your weary head into my wounded carpenter hands, and rest. When you feel the annoyance and anger rising toward your husband and children, overcome those evil voices within you by loud praise and song.

"Be like my Mother, Mary. Begin each day saying, 'Behold the handmaid of the Lord, be it done unto me according to thy will,' and then like Mary and Joseph talk to me all day."

Paula felt much amazed and refreshed by these thoughts, which seemed so different from her usual unhappy reflections, that she was sure they came ultimately from the Spirit. After her walk on the beach she had coffee with an old friend. This woman was also a mother with many children and she had lots of practical suggestions about how to make housework a little easier, such as making a schedule of jobs and tackling one big one each week, one small one each day, etc; making the beds first and dressing pleasantly so you don't feel ugly and depressed; assigning a special place for everything; putting the kids on a chore schedule and holding them to it; working at some task immediately instead of wasting a long time grumbling and not doing it. She also suggested that Paula have definite scheduled times to get away to be by herself or to be with other adults.

When she got home the house was in a terribly chaotic state. The baby-sitter had let the kids run wild and Paula had a very hard time trying to put any of her new ideas into practice; but little by little a new sense of wonder about ordinary parts of life like vegetables and flowers deepened in her life, and sometimes she would find she could talk to Jesus while she worked and that made her very, very happy. When problems seemed overwhelming she would take a little half-day vacation from the house and really speak to the Lord about her life until she could see it as a work of love for her family in Christ who loved them all so dearly.

B. Work That Is Ambition-directed and Greed-oriented

Robert is a busy advertising manager in a successful business. He came from a poor family and he worked his way through college by doing menial jobs full time and going to school at night. He studied psychology because he wanted to understand people, but then he discovered that he could use psychology in business as a way to figure out what kind of ads would really sell people.

When Robert was in high school he was very religious. He still goes to Church regularly and he married a very religious Catholic girl, but since he left college to work in advertising he finds that his relationship to God is very "basic." On his way to work he asks God to take care of the family and to give him good health so that he can make a lot of money and be sure his kids don't have to struggle as hard as he did to get through college. He rarely thinks about God. He joins in mechanically to the grace said at dinner and seldom participates in family prayer since he almost always works overtime or entertains clients in the evening.

What really fascinates him is his work itself. He is amazed to see how gullible the public is when he manages to direct an advertising campaign in terms of their weaknesses: their vanity, their fear, their greed. He enjoys the feeling of power when the sales go up due to a new gimmick he has figured out. He pictures himself continually being promoted and finally starting his own advertising company. This is his greatest dream and he will work any number of hours to achieve it.

By next year he will have earned enough money to move into the classiest suburb in the area: a place his parents never saw or even dreamed of living in. At family gatherings he enjoys talking about his work and comparing his status and success with the struggles of his cousin who never went through college and still lives in the old run-down neighborhood.

If someone told him that he was an idolator he would be amazed. He thinks of himself as a good Catholic since he never commits any obvious big sins and supports the parish. He's never heard a sermon against his life style — a manner of living which pretty much corresponds to that of the other men in the Church he attends. But his life is a form of idolatry, for all his working hours are spent in exploitation of others for the sake of the idol of status and conspicuous consumption.

To see how un-Christian his work life is we have to notice the fact that he never thinks of his clients as Children of God — his brothers and sisters — but instead as people to be manipulated. They figure not as men and women with immortal souls destined to dwell together in a kingdom of love, but merely as one figure in his success equation. Any person whom Robert meets in his capacity as advertising director could be an obstacle or a tool, a stumbling block, or a stepping stone; and it is up to him to calculate swiftly what the chances are of making this encounter profitable to himself. The extent to which such manipulation can go is to be seen in the practice among some businessmen of instructing their wives to flirt with the clients as part of the warm-up for the sales pitch! (Such an attitude could be contrasted to the way in which a genuinely Christian businessman would invite a client to dinner out of compassion for his loneliness in a strange city.)

Another way to detect creeping idol worship in the sphere of ambition is to see whether a person could imagine remaining at a lower salary in order to have more time to be with the family or for charitable projects rather than constantly seeking promotion at any cost.

It might be important to ask the question: what would make me sadder — to lose my job and have to suffer the stigma of un-employment with its sacrifices or to be rightly judged by others to be a shrewd manipulator? If losing the job seems worse than losing the right to be known as a good Christian, then we have fallen into idol worship even though we retain our connection with the Church and call ourselves Christians. The words of the Lord come immediately to mind:

"What profit does a man show who gains the whole world and destroys himself in the process?" (Mk 8:36).

"You cannot give yourself to God and money" (Mt 6:24).

Usually there is no way that the Lord can reach such a person to help him until his idol is shattered and he realizes that he has become a shallow miserable person in spite of all his status and success. Then the Lord can appear to him with open arms as did the father of the prodigal son and show him how to use his intelligence in the service of the true kingdom rather than for the sake of vanities. The way in which the work atmosphere can change once it is done in the service of the Lord will be described after some comments on the third way in which the work situation can become un-Christian when divorced from the influence of the Holy Spirit.

C. Work As a Place of Irritation

Peter does not find his work to be an exhausting burden as Paula did, nor does he strive for status. Peter works as a shipping clerk and his main desire is to do as little as possible to earn his low salary.

Since the work is rather mechanical, Peter finds that his mind is mostly on his relationships to the other workers in the office and especially on the manager of his department who is a very domineering character and who seems to just look for opportunities to criticize everyone under him.

Let's suppose that Peter's section manager has just passed by and made a nasty comment about his laziness and carelessness which led to a mix-up in the shipments. And let's say that it really was Peter's fault. (It is interesting to note that generally we get much more upset when the criticism is right on the mark since this stings our pride; whereas if the negative remarks are totally unjust, we just decide the person making them is crazy and shrug it off.) Now what is the typical way that Peter will react to such comments by the manager? Before reading the list below, think about a comparable situation in your own work situation and see how you would respond.

a) He will start defending himself, pretending he is not at fault.

b) He will find an opportunity to talk to a buddy who will be sure to take his side.

c) He will think up insults he could have thrown back at the manager. He will enjoy a fantasy about the humiliation and defeat that he could cause "if he had bothered to answer back."

d) He will build up a caricature of the section manager and describe these faults as often as possible to the other workers and to his friends.

Perhaps,

e) he will gnash his teeth and curse;

f) he will become nasty to everyone else that passes, even insulting them for laziness also;

g) he will be mean or even brutal to his family when he gets home.

h) Over a few beers, he might admit to himself and to a close friend that he really was careless.

i) Conceivably, but not likely, he might realize that it was un-Christian of him to react to a just criticism with so much anger; to spread bad feelings towards the manager, who was doing his duty, and to take it out on his family.

j) Very improbably he might actually ask pardon of some of the offended parties.

At Peter's warehouse the workers are pretty much divided into two groups: the ambitious people who flatter the bosses and want to get ahead and the regular guys like Peter who just work because they have to but do not pretend to care about the business or the bosses. Even though Peter is a pretty nice guy with his family and friends and his fellow workers, he finds it perfectly justifiable to make the most uncharitable comments about the men in the other category. He calls them names, makes fun of them either by private jokes or simply by mocking glances, and he positively enjoys any setbacks to their ambitions. It would seldom occur to him to apply to himself the admonitions of St. Paul:

"What I say is this: let the Spirit direct your lives, and do not satisfy the desires of human nature . . . What human nature does is quite plain . . . People become enemies, they fight, become jealous, angry and ambitious. They separate into parties and groups, they are envious . . . I warn you now as I have before: those who do these things will not receive the Kingdom of God'' (Gal 5:16-21).

In the same letter St. Paul also speaks about not irritating one another. Here are some brief examples which probably apply to your work situation. You know that someone would like you to do some task in a certain way. It is just as easy to do it that way, but you refuse. You even slightly enjoy the fact that you know this will irritate the other person because you want the satisfaction of doing it your way. Another example: You know that someone else wants to use the phone at the office, but you chatter on and on with a friend. Why do we insist on acting this way? I think it is because we want to be the one who dominates the situation, sustaining the image that everything should revolve around us. On the contrary, St. Paul says that love does not insist on its own way.

When we think about how many facets of our work life can become un-Christian we shudder, but we should not despair because the same passage from Galatians mentioned above also describes the Fruits of the Holy Spirit which can lead to renewal of work:

"The Spirit produces love, joy, peace, patience, kindness, goodness, faithfulness, humility, and self-control" (Gal 5:22-23).

I will briefly describe each Fruit of the Spirit, and as I do so you might want to check off the ones you feel a special need to pray for in your work situation.

Love: The obligation to love your neighbor as yourself clearly applies to all the people you encounter in your work situation. At the present time your relationships to them are probably very mixed. For example, suppose you are a shoe salesman. Maybe you have a close relationship to one or two other salesmen in the store. You are probably friendly to some of the customers. What about the lady who tries on fifty pairs of shoes? Do you feel justified in being angry, impatient, or insulting to her; or do you try to figure out why she does this (maybe she's lonely and has nothing to do all day)? Do you talk to her and make her feel a bit happier? Whatever the situation, every person you come in contact with should feel a bit happier because they have met you.

Of course we cannot just paste on a loving smile, though some companies demand that their sales people smile and say hello as a public relations device. If it is to be an overflow of Christian charity, our smile has to come from an attitude toward each person which says, "You are a human being and this is more important than petty aspects of the situation we are in." That such an attitude is really possible is shown by different people we meet who live in such a way. There is a checker at the grocery store that I go to who is known all around the neighborhood because she emanates a personal sense of concern for everyone who comes through the line. I am sure I am not the only person who picks her check-out counter even when the line is longer just to get that lift that comes from her smile.

Joy: Whereas grouchiness and grumbling have been called the smog of the interior life, joy is the fruit of a peaceful acceptance of our work and a desire to be grateful for whatever good God sends us in it — a salary, friends, benefits. Joy is always fostered by gratitude and appreciation. I can show appreciation for everything good in my work situation by telling the people around me and praising God for it, or I can resent everything about it. Such a joyful approach is not a matter of temperament; it has to do with a total response to God in relationship to the basic fact of having to work. Pope Paul in his encylcical *Populorum Progressio* says that "every worker is, to some extent, a creator — be he artist, craftsman, executive, laborer, or farmer. Bent over a material that resists his efforts, the worker leaves his imprint on it . . . When work is done in common it brings together and firmly unites the wills, minds and hearts of men. In its accomplishment, men find themselves to be brothers."

Peace: We must allow the strong spirit of peace to work in us through prayer to the Holy Spirit. The fact that we desire feuds more than peace shows how little we cooperate with grace in this matter. Our peacefulness comes from the fact that having partaken of the spirit of opposition and group factions we have reason to fear, for we meet hostility everywhere.

It is not too late, for the Spirit says "Behold I make all things new" (Rv 21:5). We can make the leap right now by praying for peace in situations at our work. Prayer is the greatest remedy for enmity, because when you pray for others you begin to have an investment in their improvement and you look for goodness instead of relishing what makes you reject them. Where there are problems of factionalism a vow never to say anything about anyone in the other groups would be appropriate.

A manager or boss can be a peacemaker in many ways. He should always try to figure out what is best to do rather than act on prejudice based on past difficulties. A boss should make criticisms in a mild way, always complimenting the person at the same time for something good that he does. Such a loving attitude will help the employee to avoid developing the talent for what has been humorously called "injustice collecting."

Patience: Christ is the Lord of time. We are building a kingdom of love for him, and it follows from this that it is more important to be patient with our fellow workers than to achieve results at the expense of great tension. This is sometimes difficult to do. Waiting for someone else to do his part is not easy. If we were eager to pray all day, as we should be, times of waiting would be welcomed as opportunities of conversing with the Lord. Enjoying such dialogues with the Lord would become the substitute for standing impatiently over someone's desk making it plain that their slowness is driving us crazy. If we are loving and patient, we will bring out the best in the people around us and things will go more smoothly than when we try to speed up their natural rhythms. But, here again, we cannot just become patient because we see that it is better. In order to grow in patience we have to let the Spirit of God fill us with peace so that we do not cling to efficiency as a status symbol, or become filled with restlessness whenever there is an idle moment.

Kindness: St. Paul says, "Love is patient, love is kind."

Some offices, some homes, some job sites are warm and pleasant because there is a good atmosphere due to many thoughtful deeds of love. To have the time for thoughtful gestures of concern for the personal needs and sorrows of other workers we have to relax our egocentric desire to see every situation in terms of our own needs. When we realize that God is taking care of us we can afford to take care of others and express it in many ways.

Goodness: The goodness of a work situation is a combination of the spiritual states of all the people in that place. Each group of people is like a little body — all the parts of which make an impact on each other. We cannot directly control the behavior of other people, but everything we do that follows the Holy Spirit will change our work for the best and make a subtle change in how others act. This is easy to see in a home situation. If the mother is cranky, she sets off bad vibrations which are picked up by each child and multiplied in their actions. If one person is truly loving, his little warm gestures begin to set up good vibrations. This can be shown to be the case in analyzing the question many workers ask each morning at an office: "What kind of mood is the boss in today?" They know that if he is in a bad mood, the whole day will go badly for everyone.

Faithfulness: We are responsible people when we are responsive to the needs on a job rather than trying to do the least. If the basic purpose of our work is good, then we should work hard at it. If it is morally ambiguous, then we should pray to find another position. True Christians regard each moment as real; to them, work time is wasted time unless they try to do their best during work hours.

The Christian is faithful to Christ in his work situation by witnessing verbally and silently. Wearing a cross, going to Mass during lunchtime, praying, having a holy picture on the desk — these are ways of showing what counts most. They are also antidotes to the tendency to act "cool" by de-emphasizing whatever is different about oneself, even one's Christian faith. It is faithless to be embarrassed about "confessing Christ before men" but proud of shrewdness, slyness, and sin.

Humility: In every work we do, we must see that what is good in it comes from God. Our own abilities come from God. Our existence each day comes from God. Persons who are deeply imbued with such a feeling will naturally avoid obnoxious boastfulness, vanity, and pride. Thanksgiving and praise flow naturally within their stream of thoughts and words day by day. They will gladly praise the talents God has given to others because they will have no stake in proving that they themselves are better. They will see others as brothers and sisters in grace. They will understand that whatever God has given others as talents is something that benefits the body of Christ, and so they will be grateful for those talents instead of envious of them.

Self-control: Some people think of self-control as keeping a tight grip on themselves. It is better described as an awareness in the Spirit in which we allow ourselves to be controlled from above by God's will, reaching above our natural tendencies and the pulls and drags of group pressure. By living on a level of consciousness which is above the hustle and bustle of the work environment we escape from slavery to it. Through our meditations, converse with Jesus, and occasional tiny breaks for prayer, we are able to direct a fresh stream of love into our relationships at work. "Pray for every occasion, so that the Spirit leads. For this reason keep alert and never give up," says St. Paul (Eph 6:18).

D. Indecision About Work

Finally, let us turn to a problem which arises especially for people who have come into a deeper relationship to Christ and wonder if the work that they are doing at present really utilizes all the talents and inspirations they have received to serve the kingdom of God.

Joan is a wife and mother with four children ranging in age from 2 to 10. She used to spend most of her time on housework and participation in parish and community projects such as rummage sales, assisting in Girl Scout activities, church bazaars, etc.

Recently Joan became involved in a prayer group. She feels a strong urge to do something vital to bring Christ to people — particularly those who are suffering from psychological difficulties. When in college Joan had planned to major in social work;

34

but she cut this program short to get married and to work to support her husband through graduate school and then to raise their children.

Joan wonders if she should go back to school and work toward a career in counseling, but she is worried about whether such a plan would involve neglecting her family.

The concepts about decision making mentioned in the first booklet of this series are certainly important in making such an important choice.

It would also be relevant to consider the distinction between:
Vocations
Ministries
Talents or abilities
Careers
Projects.

Joan's vocation is to be a wife and mother. She may have a ministry of counseling. She probably has a variety of talents and abilities in art, music, mathematics, etc. If she goes into a career, she would choose social work. She is immersed in countless projects at Church and in the community.

As Joan decides in prayer what she should devote her energies to she should consider certain basic Christian principles which come from centuries of spiritual direction within the church.

a) A person's *vocation* is paramount in terms of his/her salvation and place in the Mystical Body of Christ. This means that one who chooses to be a wife and mother is very rarely following the Spirit if she decides to neglect the basic needs of her husband and family. In most cases a priest would betray his vocation to the People of God in their sacramental life if he spends most of his time on projects or in a career unrelated to the ministry. Many times people become so discouraged about their basic vocation that they gradually give more and more time and energy to careers or projects while neglecting their calling. In this way they follow their own inclinations instead of the inspiration of the Holy Spirit; and even if the work that they do is good for society, they will have failed in what is most important.

In the case of Joan, it might be good to decide to work slowly toward a career in social work by taking a few courses each year toward her degree, but postponing full-time work until the children are all in school — to avoid the possibility of having too little time to give them love and attention.

b) There are many *ministries* in the Lord. A service to the Christian community can be just as important as any career. Many people discover that their greatest fulfillment comes not from their jobs but from their ministries. Sometimes it is advisable to develop a ministry into a career, as in the case of a business man who does volunteer work as a Big Brother and then decides to do social work professionally in the ghetto; but many times an individual would be following the Spirit by insuring his livelihood in a nonpressure position and devoting more and more of his best energies to a ministry. A man may decide to work part-time as a mechanic and devote a good two hours a day to a ministry of prayer. The renewal of prayer life going on in many Churches today is very favorable to such a development; it may result in a combination of the active and contemplative life which will be deeply satisfying to lay people. Such a life is especially feasible in the case of men and women whose children have grown up and who find themselves with much more time on their hands.

Joan, the woman we are taking as an example, might come to the conclusion that she would be happy in the exercise of a ministry of counseling in the neighborhood informally over coffee or in her prayer group. She would be doing this without reward, for Christ; and she might rejoice in the fact that her husband's income is sufficient for the support of the family which allows her to be free of the pressures of a career. She might spend quite a bit of time reading books in the area of counseling and prayer to gain new insights; and in so doing she will also be preparing herself for a later career which might become necessary or desirable. Such a ministry exercised in the neighborhood without conflict with her family life would also benefit her own children and husband, since she would apply the insights she gets in prayer and reading to their problems.

c) Many people find that the development of a certain *talent or ability* gives them greater joy in the Lord than any career could do.

Joan may love to paint but have no hope of making it a lucrative career. As she draws, she feels she is "tracing the Lord's design of nature." She prays as she paints, and her delight in beauty permeates the whole house. She should be encouraged by her family in her painting, and they should never make her feel that she is wasting her time unless she can sell her paintings. The Lord has given her the talent and he rejoices in her exploration of it.

d) If Joan decides to embark on a *career,* she should try to discern in prayer what work really helps to build the kingdom of God and what use of her talents might have a negative effect on the community. For example, being a personnel director of a company that is devoted to something morally negative would be a misuse of her talents. If there are policies in an organization which are against her conscience but she feels she may eventually be able to change them, this situation must be pondered very carefully. One Catholic social worker I know works in a half-way house in which it is the policy to suggest to young girls birth control devices and abortion as a follow-up. My friend does all she can to try to influence the other counselors against such an un-Christian attitude. If she finds that she cannot succeed in bringing about a change in the directives of such an organization, then she will have to decide whether the good she is doing makes staying worthwhile, or whether she should seek a position which is more consonant with the will of God.

A Christian should never think that the necessity of having a job justifies participation in anything clearly evil. Otherwise he may become a building block in the kingdom of Satan instead of God. This was the case with Christians who became involved in concentration camp work in World War II in the belief that it was more important to have a good job than to stand up for ethical principles even at a risk.

e) The life style of many American mothers and fathers involves being pressured into countless community and Church affairs which often have very little result compared to the energies expended. Many times prayerful reflection on vocation, ministry, talents, and careers leads to a diminishment of involvement in short term *projects.* I do not think that our Lord wants us to do things only because others pressure us or to fill in spare time. If we have so much spare time on our hands we may be called to develop our talents or ministry to others in a more meaningful way. I do not mean to imply that it is a waste of time to help out in fund-raising events in the school or parish, because these are works of charity, but the degree of involvement ought to be subject to evaluation in prayer rather than taken for granted.

Sometimes what begins as a project that we are pushed into by other people can become a real ministry. Joan may have become a Girl Scout leader just because there was no other mother to take the troop. Once immersed in the project she might find that she is in contact with many girls who have been neglected by their parents or who have problems at school and home. Her informal counseling of these girls might become a mission of charity instead of a weekly chore.

Joan must decide about her life work in terms of prayer and reflection. A factor which often is played down but which I think ought to be very central is the simple question of what sort of activities she really enjoys. God loves us. He wants us to be happy. Unless something that makes us happy is in conflict with a prior vocational commitment, or is actually sinful, we should not suppose that it is selfish to choose to do what makes us feel good. Generally, our joyful feeling is an indication that we are utilizing the talents and gifts that God has given us to develop for the sake of the kingdom. "God loves a joyful giver," and he is certainly not gladdened when we turn ourselves inside out to do something beyond our ability just to prove that we are unselfish.

To summarize, when we feel unsure about what work the Lord wants us to do, we should go into the place of peace and pray for the guidance of the Holy Spirit. We should consider all the pros and cons in the light of such principles as these: primacy of vocation over other commitments; ministering to others as a worthy work of love even if it is unpaid; talents and abilities as gifts of God to be explored not diminished as mere luxuries; careers to be measured by the way they build or detract from the kingdom of God; and passing projects to be evaluated in terms of real results rather than by the pressure of others who need personnel.

"The Spirit has given us life. He must also control our lives" (Gal 5:25). The Spirit is the leaven of newness in our lives. Our situation is the dough. Let Christ come into every moment of our lives. "Whatever you do at all, do it for the glory of God." Let Jesus flow into the desert of our work to make all things new.

SUGGESTED PRAYER EXERCISES

1. As you go about household work, ask the Spirit to draw your attention to whatever is good in it — such as the beauty of vegetables, wood, color.

2. Thank God for your job, for the machines you use. You might call them sister and brother as St. Francis spoke of water and grass.

3. See the connection between each item of work and love. For instance, you could see cooking or shopping for food as a visible sign of love for your family. As you do the work, offer it for each person who will benefit from it, praying for the person whose chair you dust, etc.

4. Do your work with Jesus, conscious of his presence, talking to him or singing as you work, if you have the voice. Play a favorite religious record while working, if feasible. Make your work an act of doing "something beautiful for God."

5. Begin your day with the prayer of Mary "Behold the handmaid of the Lord, be it done unto me according to your will."

6. If you work with other people, ask the Spirit to show you delightful elements in each one of them: from the color of their eyes to the swift movements of their hands, etc. Be sure to fill your conversation with your appreciation of everything good others do, especially if they are part of the "other group."

7. Check yourself to see which you exercise more — the works of human nature: separation into groups and parties, enmity, jealousy, anger, ambitiousness, pride, and provocation of others; or the fruits of the Spirit: love, joy, peace, patience, kindness, goodness, faithfulness, humility, self-control. Pray for the diminishment of one fault and the development of one virtue in a

continuous way, asking other people to pray for you in this respect.

8. If you are undecided about your vocation, ministry, career, talents, or projects, pray over these decisions, taking as much time as you need for reflection.

PASSAGES FROM SCRIPTURE

"Wake up, sleeper, and rise from the dead! And Christ will shine on you. So pay close attention to how you live. Don't live like ignorant men, but like wise men. Make good use of every opportunity you get, because these are bad days. Don't be fools, then, but try to find out what the Lord wants you to do" (Eph 5:14-17).

"Keep your life free from love of money, and be content with what you have; for he has said, 'I will never fail you nor forsake you '" (Heb 13:5).

"Do nothing from selfishness or conceit, but in humility count others better than yourselves. Let each of you look not only to his own interests but also to the interests of others. Have this mind among yourselves, which you have in Christ Jesus, who, though he was in the form of God, did not count equality with God a thing to be grasped, but emptied himself, taking the form of a servant, being born in the likeness of men. And being found in human form he humbled himself and became obedient unto death, even death on a cross. Therefore God has highly exalted him . . . . Do all things without grumbling or questioning, that you may be blameless and innocent, children of God without blemish in the midst of a crooked and perverse generation, among whom you shine as lights in the world" (Phil 2:3-15).

"Bid the older men be temperate, serious, sensible, sound in faith, in love, and in steadfastness. Bid the older women likewise to be reverent in behavior; not to be slanderers or slaves to drink; they are to teach what is good, and so train the young women to love their husbands and children, to be sensible, chaste, domestic, kind and submissive to their husbands" (Ti 2:2-5).

"For lack of wood the fire goes out; and where there is no whisperer, quarreling ceases. As charcoal to hot embers and wood to fire, so is a quarrelsome man for kindling strife. The words of a whisperer are like delicious morsels; they go down into the inner parts of the body" (Prv 26:20-22).

CHAPTER THREE

YOUR CONVERSATION
IN THE SPIRIT

"Let no evil talk come out of your mouths, but only such as is good for edifying, as fits the occasion, that it may impart grace to those who hear" (Eph 4:29).

This passage of St. Paul seems to me to summarize for us how we follow the Holy Spirit in conversation. I will comment on each of the four clauses of the scriptural passage separately giving concrete examples from daily life which illustrate what the Holy Spirit is teaching us about conversation.

"Let No Evil Talk Come Out of Your Mouths..."

Under evil talk I will include nastiness, sarcasm, backbiting gossip, swearing, immoral sexual talk, superstition, egocentricity, and foolishness.

Nastiness and Sarcasm

Many Christians who would rarely swear or talk in a sexually immoral manner allow themselves to speak uncharitably to others. Some of us do this unconsciously. Others of us justify it as a way of letting off steam about situations we resent. We may also fall into the habit of sarcastic replies or comments under the guise of humor.

Such unpleasant conversation may seem to us to be quite natural because "everybody does it," and "it's only human." But when we decide to yield up everything to the influence of the Holy Spirit because we want to become new men in Christ, we realize that many natural human responses are contrary to the leadings of the Holy Spirit. If we measured everything we say by the criterion of whether or not it builds up the kingdom of love "on earth as it is in heaven," we would soon realize how unloving, nasty, or sarcastic many of our comments really are.

Gossip

Under evil talk should be included not only face-to-face, subtle, or open insult, but also that verbal combat we engage in behind people's backs. By denouncing the faults of others to *our* friends, *their* friends, and even strangers, we accomplish many evil things at one blow. We try to destroy any sympathy the listener might have for the person being attacked. We attack rather than forgive the person who provokes us, and we enjoy a proud feeling of superiority gained by putting down the other.

This may seem like a harsh appraisal of gossip which is often done just for "fun" among friends. It is true that not all gossipy conversation is as full of animosity as just described, but even so the dividing line is very thin. What one person says in fun may cause others to scorn someone who needs to be understood more deeply.

In his book *Works of Love* the great theologian Søren Kierkegaard says that he would rather face the day of judgment as a murderer than as one whose years and years of gossip succeeded in eroding friendships and insidiously corrupting the hearts of the innocent who wish to see good and not evil in the people they meet.

The very un-Christian nature of gossip will become even clearer when we contrast it later to edifying conversation.

Cursing and Swearing

Many persons in past ages considered taking the Lord's name in vain to be sinful, even if they did it out of anger or habit. In our times, however, many consider it to be harmless.

Suppose you made a list and discovered that you actually use the word "God" far more often in idle cursing of obnoxious people and annoying situations than you proclaim the name of the Lord in joy, praise, and petition?

Can it be that we are too self-conscious or afraid of the opinions of others to praise the Lord out loud but not ashamed to swear in front of others?

Suppose things were so arranged, in science fiction fashion, that the moment we said the word "God," "Lord," or "Jesus," a little bell rang in heaven and God jumped up from his chair only to see a sign popping up into the clouds: "False alarm, only a curse, go back!"

"Well," we might say in excuse, "God is not a tyrant. He knows our weaknesses and pays no attention when we fall into bad habits." Certainly God knows us through and through and takes less offense at habitual faults than at premeditated evil. Still, God wants us to be full of the Holy Spirit all the time, and no one who curses even out of habit can be following the Spirit. Think how joyful you would be if everytime you felt like cursing you praised God instead!

Sexually Immoral Conversation

Under this heading we would obviously mention descriptions of sexual acts for the sake of vicarious experiences of lust. Also to be included are lewd jokes.

But many contemporary habits of conversation fall under evil talk which are subtle enough to avoid immediate detection by the one who falls into the habit of talking in a particular way about sexual matters.

For example, many people enjoy seeing double meanings in every sentence. This seems harmless but let's think about it. Could anyone really consider that such innuendos build up an atmosphere of Christian purity?

How about girl-rating or boy-rating in which people of the same sex give a rating of sexual attractiveness to each person that passes? Can we really claim that we are following the leading of the Holy Spirit in such conversation? If we were aware of Christ's presence by our side, would we share with him our sexual rating games?

We can see how unsatisfactory such conversation is if we compare it to the attitudes and talk of a really pure person. I do not mean a Puritanic person who thinks that everything sexual is animal or ugly, but a truly pure individual who thinks that the spiritual element of love should be emphasized in any personal dealings with others. Did you ever see the way a deeply pure person looks at people of the opposite sex? His/her glance is full of appreciation of the charm of the other person. It is not cold and withdrawn; it is a look full of deep reverence for the spirit of that person. If you have ever had someone look at you that way, it reminds you of nothing so much as the way Christ must have glanced at people. Such an expression must be the result of a life of prayer which gradually excludes immoral attitudes and talk,

46

and which creates around the person a Christian atmosphere which is incompatible with indecency.

How about our inner conversations with our own selves? Do we find ourselves writing an imaginary script within our own minds in which we are leading characters who say and do impure things we know it would be sinful to act out in real life? Shouldn't we yield our inner conversations to the Holy Spirit lest we find ourselves conversing with the Evil One?

Superstition

Evil talk also flows from superstition. Nowadays we find many people dabbling in superstitious works which range from the use of horoscopes to fortune telling, and belief in mediums and witchcraft itself.

The Church has always frowned on such activities, because for the Christian Christ is the only Lord of one's life. For the devotees of psychic powers the ego is the center, and spiritual power is used to enhance the ego.

Here are some typical phrases we may use in conversation which reflect, however mildly, a superstitious mentality rather than the following of the Holy Spirit:

"Good luck, my friend." Why not say, "God bless you," or, "God be with you?" Does the Christian believe more in luck than in providence?

"I'd better not do that. The horoscope for today (or my fortune teller) warned me about this." Do we consult the horoscope page or the fortune teller about the future, thus opening ourselves to the wiles of the devil? Isn't Satan pleased that we trust in man-made systems instead of in Christ when we are anxious? Shouldn't we read Scripture and seek wisdom and counsel from Christians when we want advice?

"I must have ESP. I keep getting these strange premonitions about things that happen." A person might very well have more psychic sensitivity than others. But does the Lord want us to use such abilities in a capricious way? I think a person who suspects that he has psychic powers ought to yield them to the Spirit and discuss them at length with a Christian spiritual director. He ought to pray for the gift of discernment to make sure that the Lord and not Satan is in control of his powers.

"I feel I must speak to my dead husband. I'm going to try a medium." Shouldn't the Christian converse with the dead in the midst of his Christian prayer rather than in a non-Christian setting in which the dead person is often thought of as wandering on the perimeter of the earth rather than being in Christ's arms? Does the Holy Spirit always want us to be preoccupied with those who have gone to a new level of existence after death instead of forming deep ties of love with living people?

That superstition is contrary to the Holy Spirit, it is necessary to remember that the Christian makes God the center of reality. His own human powers are gifts given to build the kingdom of God, not powers to enhance himself or to give him an advantage over others. The dabbler or initiate in the psychic cults reverses this order. He is the central figure.

In many situations we have an opportunity to meet people who do not share our Christian faith. We ought to be witnessing in our conversation and acts to the beauty and peace of a God-centered existence. If we fall in eagerly with other people's superstitious interest in horoscopes, etc., or if we talk about our own spiritual gifts with the same kind of emphasis on expansion of the powers of our own egos, we fail to make Christ present in that situation even though we may often talk about religion. It will seem to some nonbelievers who are involved in superstitious practices that they have their own supernatural sources of power and we have our God who does our bidding. Instead of such an impression, they should be amazed that we believe that we are in touch with an utterly lovable, supernatural, transcendent source of joy whom we follow, whose bidding we wish to do, who lifts us out of immersion in self and our plans. We must emanate to others the feeling that Christianity is our salvation and theirs — not because it turns us on but because it is an encounter with a being so much greater than ourselves, the God of love, adored for his own sake.

Egocentric Conversation

As an experiment, ask yourself this question: How many of your sentences start with the word "I"? How many start with "we" or "you" or "the Lord"?

The results of such research may disclose that you are much more wrapped up in yourself than you imagine.

When Christians enter into conversation where the purpose is other than merely exchanging practical information, they should show love for the Lord and for others by praising God and by a genuine loving interest in the affairs of the other person rather than rattling off a "newsletter" about personal activities.

Of course, there are times when the Holy Spirit leads us to seek counsel of someone and to lay our souls bare and describe all that is going on within us. But most often in conversation, the Holy Spirit would have us open to listen to the spoken and unspoken needs of others, not to take the center stage and make everyone listen to us.

Foolish Talk

It is very relaxing and enjoyable to let go and kid around in conversation. Sometimes we can do this among close friends without offending the Holy Spirit. Very often, however, as we let go of our "official" pose, or our tense work-self, we also let go of the Holy Spirit. We forget that our tongues should be yielded to the Spirit.

Three ways that foolish talk can lead us to depart from the Holy Spirit are:

Saying something by accident which hurts someone's feelings; adopting a scoffing attitude toward life; ignoring a serious need for help because we are in a buoyant mood.

1) How many times do we have to say "I'm so embarrassed. I was only kidding around and I hurt her feelings so badly." or "I was joking about people of that nationality and I didn't even notice that Phil 'X' was listening!"

When this happens isn't it because our attention is so fixed on the joke we are telling and the nice feeling we have when everyone is enjoying our manner of presenting it that we just lose awareness of the special sensitivities of those around us? A person yielded to the Holy Spirit sees people more and more as God does. When he looks at a person he doesn't just see him as an audience for his jokes but as a many-layered personality with hidden wounds that must be healed rather than scratched open by thoughtless words. Therefore the Christian must not foolishly plunge into a joke or an anecdote without considering who is listening and the effect his words may have.

2) There is the possibility that much bantering conversation will lead us into a scoffing attitude toward others. If we have a group of friends who love to hear amusing stories, we will use them as raw material for our anecdote collection. We may find that we have a ready collaborator in the Evil One who would have us find the most serious things boring because they are not amusing enough for exchange over coffee, and the most sinful things delightful because they contain some entertaining feature.

3) Once we become so immersed in foolish conversation we may fail to realize that someone near us is in need of real help. Have you ever had the miserable experience of coming to someone when you are burdened with an anguishing problem only to find that the person you looked to for advice and counsel was so caught up in telling funny stories that you couldn't really get his attention? Maybe if you had broken in rudely and said, "I must talk to you seriously," he would have stopped his foolish talk, but you hoped he would sense your trouble right on your face and reach out to you.

It may seem that these warnings against foolish talk imply that the Christian should be ultra-serious and solemn in conversation. I don't think so. We should be joyful always because we know that God's love is more important than our disappointments and failures. We should be buoyant and laugh at ourselves when our false sense of self is shattered or when something really funny happens to us and to others. But, at the same time, we should never lose touch with the Spirit and just lapse into foolish jesting without concern that we might hurt someone who is sensitive about a situation, or become scoffing about things we should pray about, or become unaware of the serious needs of others.

"But Only Such As Is Good for Edifying..."

The word "edify" sounds slightly pompous, but it has a deep beautiful meaning: "to build up." As Christians we should want everything we do to build up the kingdom of God.

We can follow the Holy Spirit's leads in building the kingdom in conversation or we can follow the more natural path of simply reacting to what has been said by others or expressing the words that come out of us spontaneously. When we just do "what comes naturally," we can easily find ourselves being argumentative, or flattering people for our own future advantage, boasting about our own successes, etc.

Basically, what the Holy Spirit wants us to do to edify others is to encourage the good and discourage the bad.

My godfather, Dr. Balduin Schwarz, describes conversation as being like a ball game. Someone throws the ball to you in a certain way. You can drop it or catch it and throw it back the same way, or return it in an entirely different way. So, if someone says "Don't you think it was disgusting the way Joe acted yesterday?" you can either catch the ball and respond in kind: "Yes, it's typical of Joe. He always does that," or you could drop the ball: "Well, I don't know. I have to tell you about something more important," or, you can send the ball back in an opposite way: "I think Joe is very tired. Maybe we could take care of his kids so that he could go off alone with his wife," or "He's such a hard worker that when other people slow things down by their negligence, he really blows up." The last two responses help build something up instead of tearing Joe down.

If someone is discussing something immoral, you can discourage the bad by interjecting a really funny wholesome joke or telling something about what one of your children did.

"As Fits the Occasion..."

Suppose what you want to say is not evil in any of the ways mentioned earlier, and is something that is edifying because it encourages the good or discourages the bad. Does that mean that it should be said? Not necessarily.

What still has to be determined is if that thought fits the occasion in terms of:

Who should say it
Why it is being said
When it should be said
How it should best be said

Let's take an example. Suppose you feel that your girl friend or wife talks too much about herself. You feel she should be discouraged from being so egocentric and encouraged to be more interested in other people.

You could just blurt out your ideas about this, as do those who keep up a running criticism of every idea, action, and motive of others, and then wonder why they are so little liked. But you want to follow the Holy Spirit of love and so you ask yourself these questions:

"*Who* should say it? Am *I* the one to tell her? Maybe not. Maybe if I tell her she will be especially hurt and think I don't love her. On the other hand, maybe she will really listen to me because she knows I love her. I better think about it."

If you decide you are the person to talk about it, then you come to the next question:

"*Why* am I telling her? Is it really because I love her and want her to be happy, more loving, and more Christian; or am I doing it because I like to feel superior by giving people free advice? Do I tend to look for situations where I can put people down with criticism because it satisfies my pride to think of others as so morally deficient? Am I like some people who constantly needle others under the guise of being helpful? Do I browbeat my friends and then become indifferent or angry if they don't change? Or rather do I pray often for them with real love and concern?"

If you discover that you have mixed motives, it is a good idea to pray for a purer motive before speaking to her. If a proud motive predominates, she will tend to be humiliated and defensive; whereas if you admonish her out of pure love in Christ she will really listen.

52

Once you are planning to speak for the right reason you can follow the Holy Spirit's guidance by asking *when* to talk about it. It is always better to talk about a delicate problem at a time when both people involved feel very loving and peaceful. If you talk about the need for change in another when you are upset with her, then you will start a fight instead of leading her to prayerful self-examination.

Sometimes we feel that we just have to let out steam when the faults of someone are bothering us. My experience is that if I let it out on the person who has the fault I am sure to start an unpleasant quarrel. If I talk about it to someone who dislikes the person I'm annoyed with, then I become very uncharitable. The only people it's safe to let off steam with are very deep Christian friends. They will listen sympathetically for awhile, but then they almost always come up with an idea about how *I* should change so that I could really help the person who is annoying me instead of just complaining.

The next question is *how* the advice should be given. The Spirit teaches us never to say anything outside of prayer. We should begin with a prayer for ourselves and for the person who has the fault. In the above example, you should pray that she may be less egocentric and that God may fill her heart with more love for others so that she may care more about their affairs.

Next you ought to make sure that the way you phrase your suggestion is in language *she* will understand, depending on her level of insight. Sometimes we lapse into the lingo of a particular group and in this way we make the person we are talking to feel uncomfortable. Suppose you have been studying psychology and say: "You know, Jane, you must have an inferiority complex which you compensate for by boosting your ego in talking about yourself. You need to be more other-directed." She may become antagonistic right away because she feels stupid since she doesn't know what you are talking about.

Here is a religious way of putting it which may be equally unsuccessful because the language is used only by one group in the Church: "Jane, you really ought to be prayed over for inner healing. You must have deep wounds which cause you to circle around yourself instead of being liberated into the Lord and the love of the community."

Such an approach may be ill-advised, not only because it is framed in a language Jane may not understand but also because it may go beyond what she can cope with emotionally.

Praying over how to say something instead of just saying it in the language we ourselves find suitable will help us to see what the real path of liberation may be for the individual we love who has a certain fault. After such prayer you may be inspired to say something like this: "Jane, last night at the party, Carol seemed hurt. I was very interested in your description of your trip but I think Carol felt you didn't care about her plans for college. She didn't say anything but I just thought she felt left out. I was reading in a book about following Christ in daily life that sometimes we can be unloving without even realizing it or doing it purposely when we talk more about our own lives than we listen to what others have to say."

"That It May Impart Grace to Those Who Hear."

If we want our conversation to be full of grace, we need to do more than avoid evil and say good things at the right time and in the right way. We also have to speak out of prayer. We should yield our tongues totally to the Spirit so that more and more it may be he who speaks through us.

I think that the experience of yielding to the Spirit in receiving the gift of tongues has a deep significance. And this not only in terms of supernatural grace but as a way of explicitly giving our speech back to its source in the Word, and being willing to utter a sound just because the Spirit wills it rather than wanting to form words primarily for the satisfaction of human purposes. The interpretation of tongues reveals that the sounds are definite words whose meanings are Biblical and personal at the same time. The meaning only makes sense in terms of the relationship between man and God, and usually it has little significance on a purely human or natural level.

In prophesy — the utterance of a word in one's own language

as coming directly from the Holy Spirit — the yielding of speech to the promptings of the Lord is even more striking.

We can consider such spiritual phenomena in the days of the apostles and throughout the ages in various forms as models of what the speech of Christians should be in essence: the words come in prayer and enunciate God's messages. Love of God's word manifests itself naturally in love of Scripture and the quoting of it when it is applicable to our human situations. The Christian is urged by St. Paul to speak in psalms and to sing hymns of praise to the Lord. Christian wisdom should fill our conversation and thus impart the grace of truth. Christ is the way, the life, and the truth.

The grace of the Lord's presence is also imparted whenever we overcome the temptation of evil-talking by means of prayer, for in so doing we let Christ live in us. We let him be the Lord of our tongues.

At this point some readers might have to confess that they would feel very self-conscious if they constantly talked about spiritual things, praised God aloud, broke out in hymns, or quoted Scripture — let alone spoke or prayed in tongues or prophesy. They would feel afraid of sounding phony, super-pious, or just plain crazy. That such fears exist is partly due to the fact that we live in very worldly times, so that even practicing Christians are shocked at the idea of bringing God into conversation except as a curse word or a response to a sneeze.

But it is certainly true that there are phony, super-pious, and unbalanced ways to bring the Lord into conversation.

What is the difference between the genuine way and the false way of conversing about God? Part of the answer lies in what has been described earlier in this chapter. An egocentric person will use the religious dimension to exalt himself or herself. There will be a tendency to boast about spiritual gifts and to concentrate more on the fact that *I* have them rather than on increased joy in a deeper relationship to the adored Christ.

An impression of phoniness or super-piety can come from lack of prudence in talking about spiritual things *as fits the occasion.* If one follows the lead of the Holy Spirit, one does not speak about things others do not understand as if they were as self-evident as $2 + 2 = 4$. One doesn't speak about intimate spiritual matters in very worldly surroundings except by a special prompting to a particularly responsive individual.

In spite of all these cautions, it must still be said that very often the fear of appearing to be phony is given as an excuse simply to avoid Christian conversation all together. Since most of us are not given to silence or discussion of high ethical matters, what this means, in effect, is that we hardly ever say anything that witnesses to Christ, we never allow the Holy Spirit to speak through us, and our conversation is often void of God and full of the world.

Some Christians would reply: "I show my Christianity by deeds not by words." Certainly it is absolutely necessary to live the faith in action; but it is contrary to the following of the Holy Spirit as the author of Scripture to ignore the countless passages about praising God, singing hymns, preaching and telling of the wonders of his grace.

For one who loves it is impossible to avoid talking about the beloved. We take it as a sign of diminishing love if a person thought to be infatuated talks less and less of the beloved. By analogy, those who love the Lord tend to reflect it in speech: "If they would not, even the stones would speak," Jesus says about the procession of the palm carriers. The person who rarely speaks of Jesus usually has begun to live his life more in terms of humanistic ethics than in relationship to a God of love.

Even if we are often unworthy Christians we must love the Lord who is worthy and true. We do not speak about God to prove our own virtue. Rather, we do so to praise him and give glory to him for his great mercy to us who are so sinful, yet not so wretched as to be unable to raise our voices with glad shouts that our Redeemer liveth.

And so, let us listen again to the Holy Spirit speaking through St. Paul:

Let no evil talk come out of your mouths, but only such as is good for edifying as fits the occasion, that it may impart grace to those who hear (Eph 4:29).

SUGGESTED PRAYER EXERCISES

1. Examine your day and keep a check list of your remarks to see how many are loving, unloving, or neutral. If you find yourself speaking more lovingly just because you are doing the experiment — praise the Lord!

2. Vow to avoid saying anything nasty to anyone or about anyone.

3. Check and see if you use the name of God more often as a swear word than in joyful praise or loud prayer. When angry and annoyed try loud praise or song as a means of release of tensions and of yielding to the Holy Spirit.

4. Try praying for everyone you see instead of forming an estimate of their sexual attractions or judging their attire and hairdo, etc. If you cannot restrain positive judgments, praise the Lord for the beauty of that person.

5. Watch and see how many times you talk about yourself in contrast to others or the Lord.

6. Everytime you speak about someone or to someone ask yourself whether your words will edify. Will they increase love in the world? Jesus is listening. Is he happy about what you are saying?

7. When you want to criticize or give advice to someone ask yourself whether it is the right occasion. Are you the right person? Are you doing it for the right motive, at the right time, and in the right loving manner?

8. Try to pray incessantly and to speak more and more out of prayer, yielding to what the Spirit would have you say.

9. Read Scripture often and let the holy words fill your conversation.

10. If you pray in a tongue, practice doing it more often during moments of the day that may usually be frustrating. If not, you might want to explore this rich form of grace-filled prayer.

PASSAGES FROM SCRIPTURE

"If anyone thinks he is religious and does not bridle his tongue but deceives his heart, this man's religion is vain . . . So the tongue is a little member and boasts of great things. How great a forest is set ablaze by a small fire! And the tongue is a fire. The tongue is an unrighteous world among our members, staining the whole body, setting on fire the cycle of nature, and set on fire by hell. For every kind of beast and bird, of reptile and sea creature can be tamed and has been tamed by humankind, but no human being can tame the tongue — a restless evil, full of deadly poison. With it we bless the Lord and Father, and with it we curse men, who are made in the likeness of God. From the same mouth come blessing and cursing. My brethren, this ought not to be so. Does a spring pour forth from the same opening fresh water and brackish? Can a fig tree, my brethren, yield olives, or a grapevine figs? No more can salt water yield fresh" (Jas 1:26; 3:5-12).

"For he that will love life, and see good days let him refrain his tongue from evil, and his lips that they speak no guile" (1 Pt 3:10).

"Let there be no filthiness, nor silly talk, nor levity among you" (Eph 5:4).

"He who speaks evil of father or mother, let him surely die" (Mt 15:4).

"For I was envious of the arrogant . . . for they have no pangs . . . they are not in trouble as other men are; they are not striken like other men. Therefore pride is their necklace . . . Their eyes swell out with fatness, their hearts overflow with follies. They scoff and speak with malice . . . They set their mouths against the heavens, and their tongue struts through the earth" (Ps 73:3-9).

"And the passers-by say not: 'God Bless you!' We bless you in the name of the Lord" (Ps 12: 9:8).

"What I say is this: let the Spirit direct your lives, and do not satisfy the desires of the human nature. For what our human nature wants is opposed to what the Spirit wants . . . The two are enemies, and this means that you cannot do what you want to do. If the Spirit leads you, then you are not subject to the law. What human nature does is quite plain. It shows itself in immoral, filthy, and indecent actions, in worship of idols and witchcraft. People become enemies, they fight, become jealous, angry, and ambitious. They separate into parties and groups, they are envious, get drunk, have orgies, and do other things like these. I warn you now as I have before: those who do these things will not receive the Kingdom of God. But the Spirit produces love, joy, peace, patience, kindness, goodness, faithfulness, humility, and self-control . . . The Spirit has given us life; he must also control our lives. We must not be proud, or irritate one another, or be jealous of one another" (Gal 5:16-23, 25-26).

CONCLUSION

That everyone seeks happiness appears to be self-evident. True, deep in our hearts we long for it, but if we observe our daily patterns of behavior we find, much to our surprise, that very often when moments of delight occur we are too busy to savor them. We do not let the good things in our lives truly make us happy.

Here are four examples of this strange avoidance of happiness:

1. A woman sees a beautiful flower in a garden. For an instant she feels joyful, but in the next moment she returns to her habitual set of anxious worries and plans for the day and forgets the flower.

2. A friend from far away comes to visit. She is a very loving and tender person. The two friends feel so happy to see each other again. For a few hours they bask in the feeling of being cared for and loved. Then the visitor leaves. No sooner is she out the door than her friend is figuring out how to get all the work done that she couldn't do because of the visit.

3. A child throws her arms around her Daddy's neck and tells him how she loves him. He smiles for a moment but quickly chases her away so he can finish his work.

4. It is after Communion at Mass. The priest pauses to allow some time for thanksgiving. A young man in the congregation feels a sweet sense of peace come over him. His worries and cares seem to dissolve in the presence of God's love. As soon as the last blessing is over he puts his mind on how to get through the traffic as fast as possible to catch the beginning of the football game on T.V.

Now let us reflect on the same situations as a person following the Holy Spirit might experience them:

1. The flower: Whenever a believer sees something beautiful

which God made, the spirit within leads to praise and thanksgiving. There is no reason why all Christians should use the same words, or any words for that matter, to proclaim their delight in God's creation, but each in his or her own way will feel the spirit uplifted to God at the sight of his glorious works. The moments of praise and thanksgiving which follow upon seeing the precious flower are not simply optional additions to the experience of its beauty but rather they perfect, enhance, and illumine the original experience. The person who looks at the flower, delights, and goes back into the stream of worries, cuts off her happiness in the bud. The person who yields to the voice of the Holy Spirit by praise and thanksgiving allows the depth of the experience of the flower to unfold. She experiences the more lasting happiness because the response to the flower becomes part of her love song with God. The passing moment is taken up into the eternal promise.

2. The visit of the friend: What a gift from God friendship is! "O how good and precious it is when brethren dwell together in unity," proclaims the Psalmist. What peace to be with someone who understands and loves more and more through the years. Moments of sharing with friends can be a real foretaste of heaven where there will be no more misunderstandings, irritations, rivalries, hidden envy, wounds of rejections, etc. Friendship is surely one of the deepest sources of happiness. In the midst of the joy of being with friends, the spirit within us swells with gratitude. We thank our friends for coming to us and we feel an added warmth as we do so. But what if we let the Spirit lead us still further into a deep joyful meditation of gratitude to God for giving us these friends, these happy times? If we do so, then we allow the fragrance of the visit to fill our day. In the Spirit, we unite our human feelings to the very source of all happiness, and so we experience not only our friend's love for us but also God's love for us.

3. The child's hug: When a child is expressing love should the father quench her spirit by his refusal to stop working on his little tasks? What would the Holy Spirit prompt that father to do? Perhaps he would be led to pause in his work — really set it aside mentally as well as physically and turn to the child, return the hug

and say, "God bless you. You are a wonderful kid. I love you." Then as he resumed his work, he could thank God for his affectionate daughter, lovingly praise God for all her good traits. In this way his daughter's loving interruption would be regarded not just as a little sweet moment or even as a nuisance, but rather something he would savor for the next hour. The experience of love, followed by gratitude to God and praise of God would make him deeply happy.

4. Communion: The Holy Spirit wants our relationship to Christ to grow continually. St. Paul wrote: "For this reason I bow my knees before the Father . . . that according to the riches of his glory he may grant you to be strengthened with might through his Spirit in the inner man, and that Christ may dwell in your hearts through faith; that you, being rooted and grounded in love, may have power to comprehend with all the saints what is the breadth and length and height and depth, and to know the love of Christ which surpasses knowledge, that you may be filled with all the fullness of God" (Eph 3: 14-19).

The Eucharist is the main way in which the participation in Christ's life is shared by us. In the privileged moments after Communion or in private prayer when we taste a small part of the mystery of God's love for us, the Spirit would lead us to remain as long as possible and not to rush away to a more superficial activity, unless, of course, we are obligated to do so by charity to our family, friends, or neighbors. Remaining as long as possible in the chapel we should experience deep thanksgiving that we poor, sinful, confused, human beings are allowed to have fellowship with the Holy Trinity in this amazing way.

*   *   *   *   *   *   *   *

In all these examples we can see that the Holy Spirit wants to lead us to the green pastures of happiness in God by savoring his gifts with gratitude, day by day, moment by moment.

You'll also enjoy reading the partner booklets to *The Spirit and Your Everyday Life:*

Prayer and Your Everyday Life
by Ronda Chervin, Ph.D.

Helps you develop a personal relationship with God. The author shows where God fits into your daily routine and how you can yield your life to him during even your most tedious chores. Includes prayer exercises and Scripture quotes. *64-page booklet, $1.50.*

Love and Your Everyday Life

Helps you strive for perfect love of God in everyday life. Dr. Chervin explains how the Holy Spirit can help you deal with imperfections (yours and others) and secure a foretaste of heaven through the happiness of human love. *64-page booklet, $1.50.*

also by Ronda Chervin

The Art of Choosing

Explains how your daily decisions affect your chance of becoming an ideal person. *96-page soft-cover book, $2.95.*

Why I Am a Charismatic
A Catholic Explains

Drawing from her own personal experiences, Dr. Chervin discusses and explains the Charismatic gifts of the Spirit; briefly outlines how each sacrament can be experienced more fully by those who have surrendered themselves to the Spirit; and candidly talks about such misunderstood topics as prophecy, healing, and the gift of tongues. This book answers many of the questions people have been asking about the Charismatic movement. *128-page soft-cover book, $2.95.*

Liguori Publications
Book and Pamphlet Dept.
One Liguori Drive
Liguori, Missouri 63057

*(Please enclose payment with orders under $10;
add 50¢ for postage and handling.)*